Asylun

CARA WATSON

INDEPENDENT INNOVATIVE INTERNATIONAL

Published by Cinnamon Press
Meirion House,
Glan yr afon,
Tanygrisiau
Blaenau Ffestiniog,
Gwynedd, LL41 3SU
www.cinnamonpress.com
The right of Cara Watson to be identified as author of this work
has been asserted by her in accordance with the Copyright,
Designs and Patent Act, 1988. Copyright © 2013 Cara Watson
ISBN: 978-1-907090-80-6

British Library Cataloguing in Publication Data. A CIP record for
this book can be obtained from the British Library.

Designed and typeset in Palatino by Cinnamon Press
Cover from original artwork 'Bitter' by David Anderson © David
Anderson, agency: Dreamstime
Cover design by Jan Fortune
Printed in Poland

Cinnamon Press is represented in the UK by Inpress Ltd
www.inpressbooks.co.uk and in Wales by the Welsh Books
Council www.cllc.org.uk

The publisher acknowledges support from Arts Council England
Grants for the Arts

LOTTERY FUNDED

Acknowledgments

Thanks to:

Steve for his love and support, Jo for giving me a voice, the Open University for their Creative Writing courses and Exeter University for Bill Greenwell's online poetry clinic, both of which along with their participants, have provided motivation, support and valuable feedback, and to Jan Fortune for much encouragement.

Contents

Asylum Seeker
    i. Birth Day
    ii. Photo
    iii. Disappearing Act
    iv. Demolition
    v. Bedroom
    vi. Asylum Seeker
    vii. Cardiac Arrest
    viii. Inheritance
    ix. Mother
    x. Sponge cake
    xi. Book
    xii. Obituary
    xiii. Epilogue

In the Beginning
    i. In the Beginning
    ii. Fox
    iii. Pond Clearing
    iv. Frog Orgy

Home Visit
    i. Mistaken Identity
    ii. Tangle
    iii. Smother
    iv. Lily
    v. Stroke

Blue Hills
    i. Auntie Lillian's Cornish Cottage
    ii. Visit
    iii. Snapshots

Journeys
    i. Leaving
    ii. In the Distance
    iii. Carrock Fell
    iv. Helvellyn
    v. The Kirkstone Inn
    vi. Resting Stones
    vii. Dawn Horse

viii. Long Meg

Stories from China

    i. Finding Place

    ii. Poetry and Fiction

    iii. Mother Nature

The Long Wave

    i. The Long Wave

    ii. Covenant

    iii. Estuary

    iv. Rain

    v. Well

    vi. Goodbye

    vii. That Morning

    viii. Thaw

Endings

    i. Night Shift

    ii. Endings

    iii. Blackthorn

    iv. Gold Rush

    v. Tonight

    vi. Losing you in slow motion

    vii. Your Letter

    viii. Suppose

    ix. November

    x. Becoming a muddy puddle

    xi. Swallows

    xii. Logos

For Henry and Roisin, with much love

Asylum Seekers

Asylum Seeker

i. Birth Day

She turns,
gathers the baby
still wet, still wrinkled.

The clatter of 1927
slips through the open window.
Bitter air

clutters the halls
where babies come
and go.

Between the lines of cots
stories begin.

ii. Photo

There you are
on the church steps
in a black and white world.

He stares from the edge,
frayed in his suit and
dead carnation.

She clutches fuchsias
that bleed into the folds
of her cold white dress.

iii. Disappearing Act

He folded his words
into silence
went to bed
in crumpled sheets.

Sometimes he cut his wages
into flakes or
scattered fragments
of her Bible.

The final trick was to
turn himself
into Jesus
on Richmond Green.

He forgot
the magic word
as he dwindled
in a haze of blue lights.

iv. Demolition

Dislodging the soft moss
she ripped grey slates
from the ribcage of rafters.

She told me
not to talk about rain.

The windows gave in easily,
splintered frames that lost their grip
on cracked glass.

v. Bedroom

Pretending to sleep
I curl with
the sheets drawn up.

Jets, thirty seconds
from landing,
rattle the windows.

The box room holds noise:
sirens, doors slamming,
the police car pulling away.

vi. Asylum Seeker

He spits
words
like lemon pips,

grabs apples
from
empty air.

Outside
grey geese
come honking.

vii. Cardiac Arrest

Cell walls lean in,
dark shapes spread like bruises.

Inside –
wires short circuit,

his mouth thickens
his shouts clot.

Light squeezes
through a cracked pane

the hole in the door
sees nothing.

viii. Inheritance

Hard wired
for heart attack

he died in a police cell.

Whispers of insanity
in the bedsit,

she threw away his stuff.

Circumstances can cause
breakdown
              of the heart.

We never mention him now.

ix. Mother

knits me a cardigan of wire wool
like a loose skin, hung
on an orphaned lamb.

I hear her whisper
while she grates lemons
into bitter cakes

bends to a steamy sink,
her apron strings a knot
of varicose blue.

She slips thread into needle,
extra strong,
stitches my lips

picks at my edges
mends me
her way.

x. Sponge cake

She shuts the front room door.
On the mantelpiece –
a row of photos like tombstones.

Tea? It isn't a question.
Strong, bitter,
how she likes it.

Remember the teapot, she says.
The one I used after your father's funeral,
when they came back? I gave it to charity.

Cake? It isn't a question.
The knife sinks through the sugar dusting,
the bright window

screens a walker in the sun
hiking the flint path
that leads away to the hillside.

You must remember? she says.
You never remember she says.
I imagine the climb, the cliffs beyond.

The sun shifts cloud on the hill.
More tea, more cake?
The tea darkens, the knife gleams.

xi. Book

The cover was mossy, dappled green,
a melt of names.
over cradling pages.

Last time I saw Dad he was in the garden.
The flowers were curling,
brown leaves falling
like commas on the grass.

We collected inside,
the silent few
and the unseen, ravenous flames.

And that was all there was;
scarcity,
a settling of ash, words
inked in a book of remembrance.

xii. Obituary

I would have written it
sitting on a mossy bench
by the estuary.

There the river breathes
a slow exhalation over
knotted bones of driftwood.

There I can see
your long shadow
across the ripples.

I would have written it
if I had not forgotten.

If I could find something to say.

xiii. Epilogue

If I ever float to the surface
riding the suck and drift of waves
like a plastic bag

or tangle in the river
with spokes and oil spills
soaked with industrial foam

my clothes filled with dead fish,
I will only need to twitch my fingers
to prove that when she said

go drown yerself
I could throw off her curse
and step from the water

In the Beginning

i. In the Beginning

you floated

washed rags of flesh and
the ivory curl of bones

snagged on a wire

breathing a sea of silk and grit
in the warmth of a rhythmic cavern

hearing the hush, hush of waves
washing the skull's hollows,

carving the broken scraps
like a shoreline

till you shiver from the water
and chilled air floods your lungs.

ii. Fox

He has stopped
on the tip of the field
frozen for a moment
in curves and lines,
catching my scent
and the echo of
boots on grass.

A museum piece;
plastic eyes, corroded fur.
My breath mists the glass between us.
With the twitch of an ear
he destroys the myth
of preservation,
throws the moment away.

iii. Pond Clearing

I'm here to the top of my boots
in water, its once clear skin
pock marked with duck weed.

Old red roots tighten like capillaries
knotted in mud
and I dredge up

sodden leaves and twigs
orange- brown from autumn.
The fresh jelly spawn

trembles at the edge like
bubble-wrapped commas,
interrupting the drag of the net.

iv. Frog Orgy

Ugly, ugly, ugly
they rasp,
puffed up in camouflage

half sunk under
the stew
of a stagnant pond

in which
they garble
invitations to the ball.

A mean Spring
wind crumples
the simmering swamp

of dancing grey-green
princes, waiting for partners,
blinking their marbled eyes.

Home Visit

i. Mistaken Identity

They've just released me from prison she says.

I look around; four walls, a bed.
The TV screen flashing pictures of
a dark-eyed, smiling girl.

*My mother died while I was away
and no one told me.*

Her face is old leather.
Through the window I see boats
anchored in Falmouth harbour.

She deflates into a chair.
Lifts her beaker with a shaking hand.

I knew they would realise their mistake, she says.
Could you take me to the airport?

ii. Tangle

Looking back I see her
bent over the steamy sink.

Now she drifts
just outside the conversation,

thinks the door should be locked,
fingers the edge of my cardigan

turns away when I leave.

iii. Smother

Her jaws unhinge,
she locks me in her world.

Chews my words
and spits them back

with ease. Spews venom
between teeth and tongue.

As she uncoils
I feel the muscles

tighten at my neck
begin to choke

as she squeezes
the life out of me.

iv. Lily

had been blind since 1950.

Now her body had forgotten
how to bend.

For a while she could lift her hand
to touch the dog.

The last time I saw her
her voice was finished,

but for a moment
she was still there

with a crinkle
at the outer edge of her eyes.

v. Stroke

His eyes were fixed,
lips silenced by his brain.

Just one hand could connect,
could lift and stroke the air

like it was an old dog.

Blue Hills

i. Auntie Lillian's Cornish Cottage

Still smudged
from the stuffy train,
trying to forget the stale fragrance
of cigarettes and coffee smears,
the city stink,

I follow the old mine track,
a fragile sun edging the distant waves.
Wheal Kitty:
that crumbling effigy of the past,
Ozymandias of the heather.

The track crunches underfoot
like dampened ash.
A fractious wind stunts trees
brings tears
to shuttering eyes.

The cottage; old, white, damp.
Perfumed with joss sticks and salt air,
goat musk and cats.
In the sanctuary I meditate.
She speaks to the dead,

blue eyes intense
with a guru wisdom,
Hazrat Inayat Khan is here.
I hold out youthful hopes,
as a sacrifice to the gods,

hear them laughing
while the dark tide
follows yesterday's moon.

ii. Visit

She knew all sorts
so when the old Sioux turned up
I wasn't surprised.

At Trevellas Porth,
feathered in sea mist,
cut in granite,

he stands like a president
in the Lakota's hills.

Warm clay in my palm,
kiss the calumet,
pipestone and wood,

breathe smoke and prayers
to the Great Spirit as

the gathering tide rattles shingle,
takes handfuls of cliff
from the crumbling cove.

iii. Snapshots

It fell from the book of prayer,
a grainy scrap of black and white,
its edges tattered.

I remember you tending the beds,
bent between bushes of
grey-green gorse that stabbed

at your bramble-snagged hands.
I remember your blackberry fingers,
your scent of earth.

*

The red cross is fresh
on your hat as you kneel beside
the men of rags and angles
dragged from the wagons,

from the shell shocked air
and the mud into
scenes shot in sepia
that you never forgot.

*

Now you are white framed
in a hospital bed,
old dirt under your fingernails
and a blur of nettles choking your garden.

The machine catches your heartbeat
like the trigger of a gun,
prints little hills
faint on the horizon.

Journeys

i. Leaving

The day is wrung out,
puddles unzipped by passing cars,

silence between us
and the tide on the estuary receding

over inlets like old, lumpy scars
cut into the mud.

Bodmin Moor curls like sandpaper
wearing down the stones

of the Cheesewring
and Hr Carwynnen.

We leave the last cairns
and barrows

hidden like bad moods
in the folds of land,

and a glimpse of Colliford
flashing a smile to the deeps of Dozmary pool.

ii. In the Distance

Scafell Pike
and the Langdales
like giants reclining

in each dip and hollow,
the slouch of hip, heels
and straightened thighs along the skyline,

elbows propping up the clouds.
The lakes gather the cold,
the steady melt of snow as

we shrink like the blur of headlights,
become slight as disturbed leaves
that spiral over the road.

iii. Carrock Fell

It's dark at four. The sun
squeezed between sky and fell

drizzling blood orange over the slope and scar.
I drive slowly; feel the squash of mud under tyres

as the headlamps dissolve the night
into a craze of raindrops.

The ponies are bunched
frames of wrought iron

their short breaths like puffs of steam
from old engines.

iv. Helvellyn

I climb for hours to Red Tarn
the clouds caving in,

near enough to touch.
I reach down to burn my fingers in the snow,

to clutch at the stones that slide beneath my feet
like beads of mercury.

Somewhere above me,
where the path is only wide enough for one

Striding Edge slices through the sky
and silent flakes melt like stories,

disappear into the lakes.

v. The Kirkstone Inn

slots into the roadside
squat as the rocks above

by the hanging tree's
crooked shadow

where sometimes
the moonlight catches

a figure that swings
and twists towards me.

vi. Resting Stones

Last night they set her a place
by the window,

saw a light

flickering low behind the cottages
an owl scattered like ash against the sky.

Now they carry her,

along the coffin road from Ambleside,
heads down,

lungs suckling the cold air.

Set the box on a resting stone,
forgetting

that they are almost at that moment
when the journey changes

when the gathering turns
from the grave

and returns,
to something else entirely.

vii. Dawn Horse

In the light before daybreak
everything is carved pumice and ash.

Come morning the osprey has returned,
wings measuring the sky
above the sheet metal lake.

The mare shifts her weight
against the heave and push
of her belly.

In the shadow of Skiddaw
she nuzzles the dark sprawl
until something stirs

until the foal stands,
top heavy as a daffodil.

viii. Long Meg

Long Meg leans against the light
bleeds sandstone into the soil.

In the lane the wind snatches at shadows
catches at ribbons that flick on the hazel

in the hiss of the midwinter frost.
Alone in the dying stain of the sun

she clutches the horizon
and the evensong drifts across the fell

like ash clouds,
bringing soft prayers to other gods.

Stories from China

i. Finding Place

We keep a dog to watch the house
A pig is useful too
We keep a cat to catch a mouse
But what can we do
With a girl like you.

Traditional Chinese nursery rhyme

Found in a thin, green blanket
by the party school
on the Zhongshan road.

Guangdong heat squeezed
smog clouds over the high rise
when you became my daughter.

Through her days in the rice field
another woman bends to the earth,
to the water,

and you a scrap of memory
like
        a book of unfinished lines.

ii. Poetry and Fiction

You like the way words are orderly,
you put them on paper
and they stay.

You read poems to me –
Timothy Winters comes to school –
show me the rhymes, the metaphors
ask if he is still alive.

Your history is Chinese red stamped,
the finding story, the orphanage notes.
There is a pretty backdrop for the photos.

I turn you away from the possible truths,
the birth control official,
the three hundred yuan,
the danger of unwritten words.

iii. Mother Nature

They give you a child
but it doesn't smile.

After waiting so long
travelling this far

it reaches out for a hug
but you don't have any.

You give it a bottle of ice
and hide in the bathroom.

It wants to learn,
rummages through cupboards

so you give it stones
and shut It in the hall.

That will teach it, you think.
It leaves a sticky fingerprint

on your skin,
so you scrub it off,

clean up the mess
give it cardboard instead.

the wrong child stares at you.

The Long Wave

i. The Long Wave

At five thirty I wake
with the taste of rust on my tongue

and rain slurs
blurring the dust on the glass.

In the last rays of darkness
I go to where we walked,

with the cries of herring gull, curlew,
sandpiper, godwit

echoing like half forgotten voices.
Go to the old ship

crisped white by barnacles,
with a scrap of leather

nailed to the prow,
as bleached and crinkled

as the skin papered to the back of my hands.
The tide sucks a slow curl of

salt mist through the hull,
like the rib cage of a whale

breathing the sea.

ii. Covenant

When the water is low on the lake
I can see the tip of the old spire
above the dark ripples and
the shadow of the dam.

She packed up their best china
before the barn groaned
and waves swam
through the gravestones,

leaving the fish
to take communion
in the stained glass rainbow
flooding their Byzantine bowl.

iii. Estuary

Elms point naked fingers,
pour broken sunlight on the path

where ash keys shatter underfoot
like frost-bitten bones.

The long tongue of the tide
licks the salt weed, the mud,

the dead wood.
For a moment I am still

in the garden of Eden
and beyond the river's edge

no one is forsaken.

iv. Rain

I called
into the space

where
air settled

where
I waited

for your voice
to appear

brief as a rainbow
on a wet road

brief as silence
between echoes.

Even after the autumn leaves
I waited,

but there was only
the breath

of emptiness
after rain.

v. Well

a shiver of light
in the water, a sixpence
spinning in the dark,
falling on its face in

the rain- scarred tunnel,
with the moon trickling
and the circle echoing,

echoing.

vi. Goodbye

She sways like a cradle,
shrouds singing in the wind
and the jib clapping.

I am left on the edge
with the slap and wash
the rush of the water

bustling like a crowd
on a jetty
hands raised in a single wave.

vii. That Morning

I went out early
while the frost
was still sizzling

and the trees
curled black,
like the feet of a dead crow.

A meteor,
fading
on its tired journey,

scattered ash
into space
and the earth tipped

towards Cassiopeia.

viii. Thaw

At midday the ice snaps the lake
the water dark under
a grey sheet that rips and shivers.

Sun stains the sky's gauze
until the light closes,
until the eclipse smothers the earth

until all that remains is

absence.

Endings

i. Night Shift

She moves away from the window
but the lightning follows her into the room
flashing like a torch,
briefly illuminating those dark corners,

like that time in the woods,
when they searched through the night
turning over the soft earth
the mulch of dead leaves, twigs,

glimpsing that curve of white
amongst the roots, a fragment of skull
or a warm fungus squeezing into the dawn
from its damp womb.

ii. Endings

The last words twist
like that rabbit the dog caught,
lying quiet
finished with the struggle.

You take a deep breath,
drag your bags to the door,
stay silent, respecting a death,
however small.

iii. Blackthorn

That last spring
we cut down the blackthorn.
It snarled and snagged
like barbed wire.
We stacked it high, ready to burn.

Over the summer it dried
brown streaked and brittle
while the grass under it
died, spreading a stain of
pale yellow bile into the meadow.

It took hours to light.
We splashed it with petrol
poked tapers into its heart
till the cautious flames
cracked like dislocating joints

and I turned from the pile,
heard something screaming,
high pitched.
Later I searched through
a drift of white ash

for the bones of some small creature
caught accidentally, as if I were looking for
a reason to leave things in place,
a reason to let the brambles and weeds
take over.

iv. Gold Rush

She bends over the pan
sees herself twirling in silk skirts

liquid circles swinging
with a rush of music and clean hands.

Her face has the moon-bright
hint of a sharp frost

but the hem of her dress
is starting to scorch, in a heat

that will shrivel and crease her
into knots and leather.

Blistered hands clutch the chipped saucer
while dance partners shuffle past

their hands aching to rest in her curves
their whispers shivering on the horizon.

v. Tonight

the dogs are restless
snapping at the heavy air.
Sweat presses creases into my skin

and darkness wraps a cocoon
around the cicada's click.
The night noses the heat

into the ocean
where I watch the lights
bright on the skyline,

the rush of the Atlantic
where a ship disappears
as casual as your wave.

vi. Losing you in slow motion

like cold that dissolves in my mouth,
the taste of breath

before the snow tumbles
and I sway on my fraying rope

hands against the rock face
like a drunk on an alley wall,

sucking in air as the rumble
fills my ears, the weight of our words

an avalanche, then
the silence while the ice settles.

vii. Your Letter

spoke of an ending.
The words float
through my sleep.

I slide the folded sheets
into my secret pocket
where the paper creases,

wears thin,
begins to tear,
and the ink fades

smudging your voice.

viii. Suppose

I woke
in the middle of my life

and found the days laid out
like postcards in an old album.

And knowing what was written,
would I turn them over

to write the message again?
Suppose I woke

and the light of the same moon
filtering down through the years

illuminated all the faded
and broken pictures,

the yellowing space
where I wrote;

wish you were here.

ix. November

and everything is past
its sell by date.

Rusting begonias
in the window box and starlings
swirl like a rush of tea leaves towards the drain.

On the fourth floor
I feel a draught of cold
squeeze past like a stranger.

Far below commuters glide, bent backed,
shimmering wet, like a shoal
into the mouth of the underground.

The pavements catch a staccato of sunlight
and the traffic on the main road hums
like an echo of that song

from the eighties,
that I heard on the radio yesterday.

x. Becoming a muddy puddle

When I am old
I will go out, out in the rain
and let the cold water wash me.
I will let the crusted earth of age
crumble mud brown
and the dust of my bones
dissolve in the slow trickle of my blood.
The stones in my eyes
will tumble off
and my shrivelled skin
washed thin by rivers of water
will sink into the weeping ground.

xi. Swallows

hurling through the long meadow
again in May, scribing
their italics
across the sky or little arrowheads
circling the collie.

Before school term finished,
before the days relaxed with chatter
they had lodged between rafters and roof.
In last year's mud thatch
they hatched this year's brood.

After the magpies went looting
I found four, scattered naked and bent
on the barn floor, beaks mute, gaping,
skins yellowed with death
like old parchment.

September and the air is undisturbed.
The dark lines of the telephone wires are empty,
the slow rhythms, the rhymes
of summer are moving across the sky
and the swallows have gone.

xii. Logos

Somewhere
        floating
             in a race
through the stratosphere

all the
      lost

text messages
          and emails
that technology

         failed
new words
     playing scrabble

writing constellations
             tracing notes onto stars
     hovering near the moon

a lexicon of

  alphabet atoms

       falling

        to appear
in the dim morning air

      mutterings
behind you

sighs on a breath
        signifiers circling

the beginning
     and…